NOT WITHOUT FLAWS

Tips on Escaping the Marital Toss

Olayinka Omowumi Oladoke

Book Completion Services Provided by:
TRU Statement Publications
www.trustatementpublications.com

TRU Statement
PUBLICATIONS
www.trustatementpublications.com

Truth. Reflection. Unity.

First Edition: May 2021
Printed in the United States of America
0 5 0 8 2 0 2 1
ISBN: 978-1-948085-57-1

DEDICATED TO MY PARENTS

My late dad, Ezekiel Oladoke Odukola,
thank you for backing me up in all ways.

***

For my Mum,
You nurtured a fighter, thanks for your efforts.

CONTENTS

NOT WITHOUT FLAWS

APPRECIATION

To All My Children
Thanks for making me a commandant of the
Divine Heritage Battalion,
I have just dug the foundation, please build
solid structures to beautify the legacy.

***

To all my destiny helpers, without you all,
this will remain a dream.

NOT WITHOUT FLAWS

ABSTRACT

It is the belief of some people that failed marriages are caused by women. Some will say, *oh she lacks patience, she is arrogant, she cannot build a home,* and lots of other derogatory remarks on single mothers. This book is an eye-opener to all and sundry about the loophole that we often ignore in our societies. All the names mentioned are not related to anyone.

Many times, though very uncommon, some faults are attributed to men by those who are related to them and could attest to their personal characters. Some may be described to be rude, proud, wicked, and so on. Meanwhile, none of the qualities mentioned above are limited to the reason why some marriages could not stand the test of time than the inability to know one's boundary in building a peaceful home. Although interference in some gender-related issues in the home, without a prior knowledge or instruction, can cause more havocs than what can be imagined.

In all honesty, no marriage can stand without the involvement of parents and siblings from both sides, but there must be a strong consciousness of how much the involvement will benefit the new family. Parents and siblings should try to imbibe in them, the fact that their once upon a time brother or sister, and even children is no longer the same person they were familiar with before, they should allow the couple to take their time to put their experiences together as one to form their own territory. That is why some religion settings do not permit having siblings living with their sister or brother after the wedding. This is because the bonding of the couple is very essential at the initial stage of their wedding.

Where the couple is left alone, tolerance,

forbearance, and understanding gains ground. Unlike when the consciousness of a sibling being around makes some issues too hard to overlook. That is, between husband and wife, alone in their house, the man is free to crack any jokes with his wife or the wife with the husband without any negative interpretation, this may not be possible in the presence of family members, especially where the norms are different.

The issue of hospitality and financial supports to families either closely related or friends is another problem that evolve like a little spark but always ends up creating a wildfire in marriages. Sometimes, misinterpretation of ideas towards attending to the extended family needs from couples often reflects hatred and wickedness. Many marriages survive this hurdle because of mutual understanding. The worst is always occurring when [1]supernatural forces are applied to gain access to the heart of either the husband or the wife. That is why prayer is very essential. Once the wall of understanding in

---

[1] 2 Corinthians 2:11

marriage breaks, the plan of causing confusion in the home is launched. Many men and women had been misled out of marriage through diabolical means by their family members out of selfish ambitions to get what they want, even when they are not entitled to it. It is therefore imperative for couples to always be in spirit and get closer to God.

Also in this book, the importance of good friends is unlocked. There will be a time in life when the only thing a storming marriage needs is the ministry of a good friend. Good friends do not envy each other; instead, they encourage each one another. Some families would have never dreamt of building their personal houses, if it were not for the intervention and motivations of few friends around them who had seen the potentials in them and never let go until they ensure their progress.

Example of such friends is the family of Benson, who saw the plights of their friends and stood solidly by them to cast the demon away from their marriage. The problem nowadays is that people do not cherish good friends any longer, except if they are rich. Your friend may be poor, but keep him/her; that just may be who you need to hold you up when you are falling.

A storming marriage, however, has nothing to do with religious affiliation. This is because there are many struggling Christian homes where many Muslims are enjoying theirs, and vice versa. Therefore, what matters in marriage is the ability to construct the formular and methods that suits the couple's lifestyle, since there is no one size fits all in marriage. What works in one home may be the bone of contention in the other.

NOT WITHOUT FLAWS

NOT WITHOUT FLAWS

Tips on Escaping the Marital Toss

NOT WITHOUT FLAWS

CHAPTER 1
Two Heads Are Better Than One

In the beginning God created the universe, the Heavens, the Earth, and everything therein. No one had seen God physically, but in the supernatural instinct both written and imagined, God exists. Although there are some free thinkers, based on their intellect either by facts, theories of their findings, or fables, they are on the other side of believing the existence of God. However, even if no one can specifically claim knowing what had happened some hundred or thousand years ago, with the few things that are visible around the universe, living things are created in genders, male or female.

What is unclear among other living things is whether or not marriage exists among them, but reproduction and replication is similar to human existence because God commanded it in Genesis 1:28-29. The holy books of God, the Bible and Al Qur'an, established the fact that God is the author of marriage. In the garden of Eden, after the creation of the creatures, God looked at the first human being among the other things he created; the man Adam whom he created in Heavenly image and said, "[2]It is not good for him to live alone, I will make a helpmate for him."

Human beings are different from other creatures right from creation. First, man was made from dust, that is, it took God some crafts and designs to make man. Although woman was not as nerve racking as man to be created, the process differed from a mere command like other creatures. [3]The woman, Eve, was extracted from the already existing bones of the man.

As a result, [4]humans' position over every other thing that was created commands dominion

[2] Genesis 2:18
[3] Genesis 2:21-23
[4] Genesis 1:26

by virtue of God's plans. [5]The companionship between the first man and first woman was immediate because of the heavenly presence and divine blessings. In the whole process of creation, God was ever present and controlled the affairs; He was happy to see the works of His hands. No wonder the Bible says, "[6]And God saw everything that He had made, and behold, it was very good."

On this note, the Bible refers to everything God had created as 'it' which means no man should hold this world or whatever it contains with too much strength. The man was given the privilege of giving names to all the creatures, including the woman made from his bone. This, as a matter of fact, established the authority of man over woman and whatever eyes can see, touch, or feel. No wonder the Bible states that [7]any man who cannot produce for his family is worse than an infidel. No wonder the troubles that usually ensue in the home when the

---

[5] Genesis 1:28
[6] Genesis 1:31
[7] 1 Timothy 5:8

head of the family is not up and going. [8]For having the privilege of leadership, all men should note that God is going to ask into details, how much every man had put into making his home.

At this juncture, after God had proclaimed His satisfaction with all of what His hands had made, He backed it up with a [9]strong commandment that most couples like Adam and Eve are taking for granted today. As a result, what seemed flawless at the beginning replicates daily with flaws. [10]At some points, one will wonder why the flaws? Some people will blame civilization, education, technologies, and hosts of what anyone cannot number. All starting from creation as results of disobedience. Perhaps if Adam never allowed a gap, absence, or ignorance of not being where he ought to be, the serpent might not have had the chance of talking to Eve, which means in some cases today, marriages will be enjoyed instead of being

---

[8] 1 Timothy 3:4-5
[9] Genesis 2:16-17
[10] Genesis 3:8-19

4

endured. [11]God will cherish a happy home where love abides.

Some couples will say, *oh we have happy homes,* just to hide their dirty lines, yet they know they still have a few shortcomings. [12]If Paul the Apostle could write about his imperfection, who on earth is perfect? Most problems that faced some homes today are not due to incompatibility, it's just the result of tares of the devil. These are possible because of some loopholes created by ignorance and or carelessness. It is always mysterious to view why two love birds suddenly turned into enemies a few years after getting married. No matter how farther or shorter the marital journey is, a lot of experiences are always attached to both stable and unstable homes.

The issue of marriage is not solely attached to a particular religion because the flaws in marriages are evident everywhere across the globe. As a matter of fact, it has no strong

---

[11] Psalm 133:1
[12] Philippians 3:12

exception on educational background. Hence, the drastic slope on the divorce curve from the elites and scholars.

God created all the creatures in twos, male and female, for the reason of replication, and that was why He formed Eve. Without doubt, God wanted men to replicate through marriage. To do this, [13]man and woman will forever be together in one accord and understanding. It is automatic. When a single man sees his ordained wife, there is always a special affection that will suddenly develop at first sight. However, out of carelessness, some men ignore such priceless feeling, either because of personal set standards, which is against God's plan. Some will say, oh I must marry a fair complexion woman when God's plan is for a dark complexion woman, and vice versa. Thereby leading to taking the wrong step at the first attempt. That first error will cause their journey to be full of mistakes until they can no longer manage or endure the wedlock.

Marriage is a course, an unending

---

[13] Amos 3:3

learning arena, and a center of self-discovery. Along the journey, however, there is no one, either man or woman, who is flawless. Human beings were only created as in the image of God, they are not God, hence the imperfection no matter how beautiful, smart, or intelligent they may be. Many couples believe that it is impossible to live a stress-free lifestyle in marriage because they have accepted their fate and adapted to consistent misunderstanding. Such couples will always be at the logger heads on every issue that has to do with them.

Meanwhile, the underlying problem may be their inability to identify and focus on individual responsibilities or roles in the homes. Actually, man and woman are meant to be a helpmate, yet there are some boundaries that require mutual understanding to cross in terms of roles in the house to avoid either of them feeling ridiculed.

CHAPTER 2
The Stormy Moments

Irede community was filled with a lot of its occupants again on a Saturday morning, when people were as well busy cleaning the environment in respect of the monthly national environmental sanitation. This was a time when people have no choice but to be indoors until 10 a.m., either by cleaning or doing anything else just in obedience to the government. On Saturdays like this, children and family members always have the chance of seeing each other in the morning, because mostly, some working-class family members are not always seen due to the hustling and bustling of the city life, which forces them to go out earlier to their workplaces to beat traffic.

The size of the community and its demography made it possible for everyone to know each other. This is because they either belong to the same group, attend the same church or mosque, or maybe students at the same school. This simply means, by mentioning a name, one out of three persons will be familiar with it. Several gossips had gone viral in the neighborhood about a critical domestic unrest in one of the houses in the community, but because it always happened at nights or in the middle of the night, some people hardly believed it, or underestimated the extent of it. But as people were busy doing their things on sanitation day, there came a pandemonium down the street. It was like a war uproar which instantly drew the attention of everyone to the site of the incident.

Alas and behold, it was 'them' again. Mr. & Mrs. Lawson are notorious fighter and street disturbance to the call. One of the passers-by commented by saying 'they can't change,' and 'I hope they won't kill themselves before something is done.' Mr. & Mrs. Lawson ordinarily are sweet people to deal with at their best moments, but once they tangled, nobody would love to be near them.

The house that accommodated this couple was adjacent to our house, and besides, the family is a longtime friend to my own family. Most often, when trouble ensues, either of them will report to my father, and he will settle it for them amicably. On many occasions their neighbors had called my father on phone to inform him about the couple's domestic violence whenever none of them had no patience of inviting my father to the issue.

Mrs. Lawson's voice was heard that early morning as she was cursing and calling her husband bad names. It was so disheartening to my mother, because of the way she had advised her times without number on the issue. Nevertheless, she picked up her phone as usual to call her to order. The phone went on ringing without being picked up.

My father came to the kitchen to ask my mother if it would be alright for him to go to the couple's house. I was shocked when my mother declined. She referred to a movie we all watched recently that showed a man who was bathed with a deadly chemical on his attempt to settle a domestic violence. She suggested that my father should as well call his friend, Mr. Lawson, on the phone the way she had been trying to call the wife. It was a welcome idea, so my father called his friend. It was on the tenth attempt that a voice answered from the other end. My father quickly said, "Mr. Lawson, leave whatever you are doing and come down to my house, please."

Unfortunately, it was Timmie, the boy who was introduced to us as Mr. Lawson's cousin, who picked up the phone. He answered, "Daddy, please come over to our house, there is fire on the mountain," it was a distressful response. My father was so confused about what to do next. He appealed to my mother to allow him to walk down to the couple's house since none of them was connected. Mrs. Lawson was still yelling and calling on the neighbors to help her. This made my father felt that the issue had involved physical combat.

In all honesty, the majority of their neighbors had concluded in their opinions that the couple had proven beyond reasonable doubt, that they are very incompatible, probably, that they were products of marriage match makers which left no chance of courtship before their marriage. They were both intolerant and lack respect for their personalities. On the other hand, neighbors believed that one of them would be the problem of all of them. Be it as it might, they have been in the neighborhood for over ten years, although initially, they were like Romeo and Juliet to those who were in the neighborhood when they were just a new couple. It became a mystery to nearly everyone of what the bone of contention was. On many occasions, according to their neighbors, this couple fight four days straight in a week, which means the marriage was under a serious pressure.

The husband would blame the wife, and the wife too always accuse the husband, all for a reason that is not known to the people around them. The question that always came to mind, especially when they had an episode, was, "How did they managed to walk themselves to the altar?" Alas, it is mysterious. The usual words whenever trouble ensues was either, 'you lack respect for me as your husband' and 'yes, because you are intolerant to your wife' these always made the neighbors incapable of pinpointing who was actually responsible for the family's unrest. This gradually became a weekly routine despite the emotional effects it has on their friends.

This Photo by Unknown Author is licensed under CC BY-SA

Mr. and Mrs. Lawson had been in the neighborhood over 10 years, in fact they moved in after a month into their marriage, which means they had become part and parcel of the community. By virtue of that, they could be regarded as one of the oldest residents. They were pleasant to neighbors except the usual dramas they seldom display to disturb their peace, although people understood that there is no perfect marriage. Unknown to the neighbors, before their marital problems advanced to create nuisance to their community, they had been going through pressure for a long time without finding a solution to rectify it. The more they managed to ignore the drastic effect of their differences, the more havoc it caused to their home.

Mr. Lawson always received sympathy from neighbors because of his gentle appearance, his humility, and sense of humor to the neighbors, and moreover, when they begin their drama, people always concluded that the wife was the troubleshooter.

The interference of some, and their irrational comments are often like fuel in the razing fire of the fights. Some neighbors were not there at times because of love, but to mock and make a jest of the couple. Meanwhile, the majority of them were going through worse situations than the Lawsons in their various homes, but they were able to control their problems.

My father, Mr. Benson, who was a friend to the Lawsons, got to the house with one other man at the same time. They were able to address the situation and peace was temporarily restored as usual. Among the consistent peace makers were Mr. and Mrs. Benson, who were my parents. Mr. Benson, my father, happened to attend the same University with Mr. Lawson when growing up. In fact, they lived in the same hostel back then, so he knew Mr. Lawson very well. Most times when the neighbors sensed any hot altercations coming from the Lawsons they always call his friend, Mr. Benson, knowing that he was always capable of curbing them. He did that again and again for years out of compassion and love for the family. He was overheard by Mrs. Lawson telling her husband to see him at home to put a lasting stoppage to the mess. To her, Mr. Benson was about to launch an attack on her in favor of her husband. She was already prepared to cause commotion on that day, unknown to both friends.

One beautiful Saturday, Mr. Lawson told his wife that he was going to visit the Bensons. She suggested going there with him to see her friend, Mrs. Benson, too. Her husband, knowing who she was, declined their going together. Instead, he advised her to either postponed hers to Sunday, or the following Saturday. As usual, the fire of domestic unrest rekindled. Mrs. Lawson said it's either they went together, or no one was going at all.

For so many years, going out together as a couple had been a thing of the past between them, so to Mr. Lawson, his wife was at it again. After a series of argument and agitation, Mr. Lawson left his home and went to the Bensons. Hardly did he realize that could be a kind of extension to their horizon. Mr. Lawson was welcomed into the home of the Bensons, a few blocks on the same street from the Lawson's.

The table had been set in expectation of their visitor, who had been a close family friend for several years. Meanwhile, after the last incident, Mr. Benson briefed his wife about the outcome, and his decision to invite his friend to share some words of courage and manly advice to help him sail through the marital storm. It was indeed a welcome idea, as the problem always gave them much concern. For the meeting, Mrs. Benson prepared a very nourishing, breath-taking meal for Mr. Lawson. Mr. Lawson, teasing his friend's wife commented about the welcoming sweet aroma of the food as he was led to the dining table.

Barely 5 minutes to settling down on the dining table, while the two friends were busy savoring a good meal on special occasions, there came a loud shout from the entrance of the house. There was no reason to guess who was there, they all knew it was Mrs. Lawson shouting on top of her voice, cursing the hosts and the husband. Mr. Benson was so disappointed with the way she rudely trespassed into his home, but as a peacemaker, he swallowed the pain and pretended like it was acceptable.

What started like a peaceful get together suddenly became a commotion, as Mrs. Lawson accused their family friend of being bias and attempting to lure her husband into having an extra-marital affair. She claimed that they were planning to match make her husband with a strange woman. She further said, "You are all master planners, you want to tutor him more about maltreating me, oh you kept a woman here for him, isn't it?"

Her claims were irrelevant to Mr. & Mrs. Benson's intention, but she had been known for being a troubleshooter. All efforts to calm her down proved completely abortive. At last, Mr. Lawson left the scene, he went back home shameful and disappointed. Although Mrs. Lawson tried to catch the attention of her friend in a bid to gain sympathy, Mrs. Benson was too overwhelmed to listen. Since none of the couple were ready to entertain her explanation, she left furiously, too. Back in their home, the Lawsons were either too ashamed, or rather, extremely tire to rekindle the fire of the domestic violence that day, or they both had sober reflection. Nevertheless, there was no verbal altercation or physical combat afterwards. Jah bless!

CHAPTER 3
If It Is Not From Me,
It Is Not True...

The reason why Mrs. Lawson disrupted the meeting the day her husband was invited for seeking a solution to their persistent domestic violence, was because she believed her husband would have poisoned the minds of Mr. & Mrs. Benson against her. She knew, among all other neighbors and family friends, this couple held her with great esteem and love. She could not also deny the fact that they were the only couple who could check on her whenever she is agitated. She preferred to share what bothered her with Mrs. Benson than any other members of her immediate family.

Mrs. Lawson was so pained with the fact that people around them never realized how emotionally she had been tortured in her home by her husband, and his immediate family members called in-laws. On the other hand, Mr. Lawson hardly believed that the love of his wife, a loving lady he agreed to spend the rest of his life within years back, could suddenly turn to the now Mrs. Lawson, a troubleshooter, nagging wife, and careless partner.

To a certain extent, Mrs. Benson was not happy with the arrangement her husband made by only inviting his friend for the meeting. She said, "Honey, do you know we were at fault for whatever happened last week in our house? As a woman, I would not blame my friend for causing a commotion that day, although she overreacted by losing her patience to that level in another person's home. You must pay for my broken plates and cups."

Mr. Benson replied to his wife by saying, "Look at you, women would always be on the same page with themselves. I did that to avoid what eventually happened. As a matter of fact, I was so disappointed in Janet." He was forced to call Mrs. Lawson by her first name. "Okay, let me know the cost of the plates and cups and I will pay."

They hugged themselves to appease each other for the stress experienced by their jolly family friends. Mrs. Benson encouraged her husband never to relent in bringing peace back to his friend's family. Another strategy was developed, and it was to invite Mrs. Lawson first to get to the root of the cause and pay the cost of solution.

Arrangement was made to get Mrs. Lawson to the home of the Benson family. She quickly agreed to visit them on a Saturday. She wanted her husband to be around too, probably because she had missed going out together with him or for her to hear what he would have to say as well. But with the previous incident, the hosts declined having them together. At any rate, she came as agreed upon on a cool Saturday.

She came with lots of fruits, groceries, and a box of brand-new dish sets. Absolutely, there was no need for anyone to know that she tried to replace the ones she smashed during her protest. Mr. Benson said, "Wow! You are such a sweet soul, thank you for all your gifts."

She was offered a chill beverage and just when Mr. Benson cleared his throat to explore the business of the day, Mrs. Lawson turned to her friend Mrs. Benson and said, "What a partial treatment! You guys were not giving me food the way you did for my husband?" Although she pretended as if it was a joke, there was more to the tone and body language.

Jokingly Mrs. Benson said, "Nevermind. We would soon hold a big party to celebrate peace when the time comes," (smiles).

No sooner than later, Mrs. Lawson was invited to the dining table for a mouth-watering fried rice with roasted chicken, specially prepared for her. She was surprised to see the level of tolerance and consideration the family possessed as she had counted herself unworthy of VIP reception. Now she was convinced beyond reasonable doubt that this couple was a family friend in need and indeed. She hungrily and quickly ate so as to have enough time to purge out her concerns.

As she was eating, Mr. Benson pleaded that his wife served his meal too, adding that the way their guest was dealing with the rice had really infected his appetite. The table became fully occupied by the three of them. Within a jiffy, all the contents in the dishes disappeared like a breeze. Then the talk began.

"Thanks for coming, Mrs. Lawson," said Mr. Benson. "Please, I wouldn't want you to be upset with whatever questions I would ask, it's just in a bid to find a lasting solution to your persistent domestic problem. As we all are aware, our friendship didn't just begin in this neighborhood. I attended the same University with your husband. Back then we were together in the church choir; in short, we spent our childhood together. If you remember, as well when you guys met, my friend told me everything. But recently, I began to feel so uncomfortable with the ways you were having concurrent misunderstanding in your home.

Obviously, you only mistook my gesture of inviting my friend here the last time, and in all honesty, it was only to see a way of resolving your issues once and for all. Be it as it might, I called you this day to listen to your plights so we can restore peace and harmony to your home."

Mrs. Lawson was so happy to hear the words of her host, she prayed that the love that had been existing in their home continues. Amidst tears, she began to narrate her ordeal. To start with, she apologized for her crazy display of impatience, to the extent of causing a crowd to invade their peaceful home. She prayed that the family found a space in their hearts to forgive and forget.

She took a deep breath and said, "My husband, the love of my life, gist partner and caring father, had changed from whom he used to be before I married him." She specifically stated that the marriage became less flavored before the first wedding anniversary, and she had been enduring instead of enjoying ever since.

With all attention, both Mr. & Mrs.

Benson gave enough opportunity required to get to the root cause and the turning point of a holy wedlock. She paused for about two minutes with tears rolling down her cheeks; she looked up, trying to catch some breath just like dialoguing within herself whether or not to open-up. All this while, Mr. & Mrs. Benson were looking at her with sympathy and imagination of the Armageddon war going on in her mind. At last, the silence was broken, and the peaceful rendezvous availed, in-depth, the problem.

Mrs. Lawson described how nice, kind, and hardworking her man was, how he would never allow her to frown her face for any concern without giving a lasting solution. Above all, she confessed her genuine love to the man in her life. However, she pointed out the reason why the story changed in the relationship. She said, "My husband is always interfering with my domestic responsibilities in a damaging way."

This was beyond the hosts' understanding, this caused them to ask for more explanation, the Genesis of it. Mrs. Lawson sighed deeply and started her story: "I met my husband at a youth camp organized by the Joint Christian Association in my community. As a young graduate and beautiful Christian sister with a strong zeal for the things of God, I was among the elected officials who were in charge of the activities slated for the camping. We were randomly selected from all over the state to ensure equal treatment for all the participants.

As a result, all officials became one big team, focusing on the success of the program. I was in charge of the kitchen and by coincidence, my husband was elected to pair up with me. Since the aims and objectives of the Christian Association included stabilizing their wards in the religion, series of talks and seminars were adopted to encourage the matured and independent participants to see the rich opportunity of getting their heavenly made partners via the camping, in a decent and Godly manner.

The closeness in discharging our responsibilities as the food machines for all the participants by and by increase a kind of affection between the two of us. I saw a very hardworking, tireless leader, and a good teammate in him. Meanwhile, he had the same feelings as well towards me. He later told me during our courtship that he saw a good prudent resources manager, and a woman with a larger heart in me, during the course of the program. Neither of us showed any sign of intimacy beyond working towards the success of our camping. However, we exchanged our contacts at the onset of the camp for accessibility to each other when necessity compels. Of course, the phone numbers became part of our contacts lists (smiles).

After a month, I received a call from him; he said it was just to check on me since it had been a while when we parted from the camp. As a matter of fact, it was a gesture that had long been expected. I was happy that he called. Shortly after the camping, I dreamt and saw myself playing in a big courtyard with a diamond ring on my middle left hand finger. As I was admiring the ring, I saw someone emerging from a corner with two glasses of wine in his hands. As he was drawing closer, I saw my now husband coming towards me with a beautiful smile. As he got a few steps to where I was standing, he disappeared. At first, I could not relate to the dream, so I disregarded it.

I had a series of dreams or what could be referred to as hallucinations, all bearing his image. When I could not bear it again, I told my mother just for motherly advice and possible interpretation. I was twenty-two years old that month. Upon hearing my dreams and the likes, my mother suggested taking the issue to our Pastor. I was too ashamed to relay my dreams how much more telling the Pastor. I quickly declined the idea with a threat that I would not tell her anything about me again.

As a mother who had probably gone through the same stage in her developing years, she persuaded me about the importance of taking such step at a time like that. I explained to her that the Pastor might look at me like a sloth, who went to the campground only to seduce men.

My mother answered, 'I won't take myself to the Pastor to disgrace myself if you had seen more than one person in your dreams. This type of situation occurs when God is revealing mysteries to His loved ones. Never mind my daughter, God will order our steps.' She assured me.

My mother was a very devoted Christian with a strong Faith in God. She believed so much in Prayers. In fact, my mother could call her Pastor to know whether it's safe to drink water. Knowing that about her, I knew I could not change her mind.

The following day at church, after the Bible Study program, she beckoned on the Pastor to grant her a few minutes to pour out her worries for spiritual supports and directions. After a long discussion, the Pastor told us what he received from God while we were talking; he told us that the man I saw in my dream was my husband, made in Heaven. He revealed so many things to us, including the danger that could evolve if we let go of God's hands. He commended on my attitude, and patience that God endowed me to face my education and brought joy to my family, and for making the church of God proud as a good ambassador.

I went home full of joy and optimism that the love bird would call again one day to confirm the dreams and the man of God's revelation. At times, I would replay his recorded phone call to hear his nice voice. I even set a special ringing tone for him on my phone to differentiate his call from other callers.

Before leaving the Pastor's office, I was directed to go on a three-day fast and prayer for the fulfillment of God's plan concerning my marital life. I did so devotionally.

On the seventh day, my phone rang! I knew the caller before picking my phone because of the special ring tone applied to his name. Picking it up, I heard him singing joyfully on the other end. Before I could open my mouth to say hello, he said, 'Sister, can you do me a favor?'

I answered, 'Is everything ok brother?'

Because I was scared to my feet. 'How can I help you?'

He continued, 'Can you please join me in prayers for interpretation of dreams? I had been having these persistent dreams about someone and it is becoming too much.'

Then I said, 'Brother, why can't you see your Pastor over it?'

He said, 'Okay, but I think you can team up with me as we worked together at the last camping program.'

Having gotten the idea, I promised to support him. Afterwards, the regular how are you doing and other greetings ended the discussion. Instantly, I felt an arrow piercing through my heart. The rest is the story of what you were seeing in us today, but for the sudden changes we began to experience after our wedding."

Mr. Benson cleared his throat and said, "Jane, to me all your story is not new to me, because I was with Raphael the day he called to tell you that he had been convinced beyond reasonable doubt that you were his wife, because we were living together that time. He so much loved you, he placed you at the center of his heart, even your picture was set as his wallpaper on the phone. We both prayed for your coming together from day one to the final day of getting married. In all honesty, the first day I sighted you, I got to know the reason why my friend was in love with you. This was the reason why this latest development disturbs me always. So, Jane, please, let me know the cause of the troubled water."

Mrs. Benson could not hold back her tears when she heard the good commendations of her husband about the couple. She knew it was the work of the devil and believed there would be a solution when the cause could be established. Mr. Benson promised to do all that it might take to restore peace, harmony, and love back to the family. The marriage would be further enjoyed and not endured anymore.

CHAPTER 4
What You Did To Me

Obviously at this point, Mrs. Lawson did not want to talk about the genesis of their problems because of the implications on her, the husband, their children yet unborn, and their families. It took her about 20 mins to break the silence. Unlike when she was sharing the scenarios of meeting each other at the camp to when they both said *Yes*. She became cold and completely unwilling to talk.

The hosts both said, "It's ok Mrs. Lawson if we have to call it a day…"

She looked straight into their eyes, sighed, and said, "It's all my husband's fault. Before we finally got married, in fact, before the introduction, I had gone to my husband's place to visit his parents more than three times, one was to introduce me to them, the second was to celebrate my father-in-law's birthday, and the third was to attend the interview and wedding counseling organized by the parent's Pastor. In all, I had always looked forward to a subsequent opportunity to pay another visit, simply because of the warm reception they always gave to me.

After our marriage, God was so gracious to us, within five months, I became pregnant. We were both happy. One night my husband came back from work, after having his dinner, he told me we would be traveling to his place over the weekend for the wedding ceremony of his cousin. This cousin was also close to me, so I didn't see any reason why I should not be there.

Being in the first trimester, I was still experiencing the morning sickness and some funny symptoms of pregnancy, but I believed I could manage it. We did not discuss it with anyone, and to avoid people from knowing, I was faking my strength and capability. Throughout that Friday, all the women in the family were engaged in the hustle and bustle of the ceremony, including me, at the expense of my fragile condition. This went on till the evening of the wedding day, just to prove that I was supporting the families.

The story changed in the night when I could not sleep. My whole body became worn out. I felt excruciating pain all over my body and started cramping. My husband was extremely tired, he slept like a man-of-war that escaped from the field. As I was groaning, I thought he would wake up to show sympathy, but alas he was deeply asleep. I woke him up after a few minutes of attempts; he opened his eyes like: *why did you have to disturb me*? But when he saw the way I looked, covered with sweat, he quickly opened his eyes so wide. 'What happened honey?'

I was too sore to talk, I could only explain with tear flowing. He jumped up! Put on his trousers and sat beside me robbing my back; yet I got more uncomfortable by the touch of his hands. It was like I wanted to vomit, excrete, cough, all at the same time. My temperature was high enough to put a bowl of water to boil, and my head was banging like the drum set. I had never seen my husband as scared as what he was that night.

He said, 'Honey sorry, I cause this, I should have let you stay behind because of your condition, what can we do now?'

Honestly, I had no clue to what could be done at that moment. It was 4 o'clock when we decided to take off back to our station. The question was, how are you going to leave the village in that delicate condition? But that seemed to be the best option, as there was no good hospital available, and peradventure I got admitted, how do we inform our offices? I remembered I had some painkillers in my traveling bag. Although I had been warned not to take such medications at that stage of my pregnancy, now it is quite inevitable. The pain was too harsh to bear. I took two tablets to suppress it. The cramping did not stop. My head was still aching, and my eyes were so teary.

Thank God we had already told the family members that we were leaving very early, so nobody suspected anything. I managed myself to the car, and we left with the hope of driving straight to the hospital. Few meters to the hospital, I felt a hot flush combined with a sharp pain in my lower abdomen. Without anyone telling me, I knew I lost the pregnancy. I told my husband what happened; he insisted that we proceeded to the hospital.

Dr. Thomas was a family friend and Doctor. He was so sad to see the first pregnancy gone. He blamed both of us for taking the risk of traveling for such an event that involved physical labor of me at that stage. He was especially mad with my husband, who thought that the custom and tradition would not have allowed me to be exempt from family activities on such an occasion. However, he prayed that we get over it soon and make another baby in due course. Medical supports were given to ensure my wellbeing. I was admitted for three days for observation and later discharged to go home and continue a bed rest for two weeks.

Four years passed by, there was no sign of pregnancy, I moved from one hospital to another for medical help, all to no avail. Many of my friends invited me to churches around the city, it was like I had committed the worst sin in life. My mother came up with a series of Pastor said *this* and *that*; fasting and praying like Mt. Everest would shift location, yet the story remained the same.

Sooner than later, my husband began to act up in the house. He became so restless, any little misunderstanding would escalate than normal, I began to feel different in my home. We do not talk affectionately like before. At times, I got so carried away to the extent of being forgetful. The pressure was coming from all around his family. No one seemed to appreciate me anymore. Some of his siblings would bump into our house and do whatever pleased them. When I tried to refuse some obligation, they would abuse me like a nobody. The worst was telling lies on me when the opportunity availed, all to poison the mind of my husband against me.

At times, my husband would realize his mistakes, begged for forgiveness, and the home would experience the normalcy. He promised to handle his family by himself to safeguard me and the interest of our home. Sometimes, the more he tried to cover up, the more he exposed me to troubles. This often confirmed the allegation levied against me that I was driving them away from our home.

One day, I came back from the office under a very heavy rain, hoping to just warm up the food in the freezer for him and myself. I met one of his uncles who was living at the downtown. They both told me the uncle came barely 10 minutes before I came in. I greeted him and made my way to the room to change my clothes. Since I met them taking drinks, I took my time to freshen up with the intention of setting dinner for all. My husband came to the kitchen to meet me and said, 'Honey, I want us to treat uncle with pounded yam, his favorite, I had already told him, never mind I would help you pound it.'

I was so perplexed. 'There is no yam at home, I had planned to stock the house by the weekend, no yam no matter how small. But why did you tell him? Anything could have been okay for him. Now how do you want him to feel about me?' I felt a warm water rolling down my cheeks because I knew what could follow. He too was so disappointed by his folly. Nevertheless, I summoned courage and set the table, this time not the food from the freezer, but another one with fresh African soup garnished with goat meat, chicken, and catfish just to compensate his expectation.

I had never heard the kind of abusive words this uncle rained on me before in my life. He left the table without tasting anything from the plates. I was expecting my husband to plead on my behalf, at least to show his fault, as a rude interference of duties. I packed the plates with a very bitter heart, watching the two of them discussing women and their crazy attitude towards in-laws.

After the departure of the uncle, I expressed my feelings to my husband and suggested that in case of another time, he should allow me to handle hospitality that has to do with food. He promised to correct himself. I cannot recall how many times he repeated the careless goodwill.

Another instance was the day my mother-in-law came to spend the weekend with us. I had never opposed her visiting us, although many of my friends dislike her frequent visitation, which at most times ended up in complaints. But as a Christian, and for the love that was existing between me and my husband, I always saw her pressure so inevitable. What if she was my mother? Unfortunately, she did not reciprocate my love, simply because she believed I was unproductive.

A day before her arrival, I was lucky to get a fresh catfish on my way from work that evening; the seller only had one left, so I bought it for the dinner. Two of my husband's friends came to visit us, and I was happy that we all consumed a rich dinner garnished with fresh fish. The whole fish went for dinner that day.

The following day my mother-in-law came, and as usual, she was bonding with her son when I walked in from work. I was so excited to see her, even though she answered me coldly. I always put a deaf ear and blocked eyes to her side when greeting her so her response would not hurt my feelings, but I would greet her with full respect and total humility. As I was walking towards the kitchen to prepare food for her, I heard my husband saying, 'Please bring a piece of that catfish for her to step down.'

I heard a sudden bang on my head out of dismay; I knew I was in for another trouble. Then I said, 'Dear, please excuse me for a second while entering the kitchen.'

In a jiffy he came in, so excited like winning a lottery, he said, 'What can I help you with?'

I replied, 'Please clean the mess you put

me in.'

Looking so confused, he asked again, 'Which mess?'

I answered, 'The mess of rude interference again.' I said, 'Did you ask if the fish still remained?' I showed him the pot that was used for preparing the fish the previous night when we had his friends in the house.

He suddenly broke down in tears; 'Yes,' because he knew it would not be easy as it was when his uncle came.

We were both glued to the kitchen, because he had no clue of what to tell his mother. He came up with so many suggestions, I felt I could not be sharing the pain I didn't inflict on him so I was just saying, 'That's good,' 'Okay,' 'Well you can try that too,' and many more. I engaged in cooking what was available, even if she ended up rejecting them. At last, he chose to take his mother out for a ride to a barbeque spot at the heart of the city just to cover up. I encouraged him to go ahead and try it.

It was so horrible hearing what was coming out of my mother-in-law's mouth that night. She shouted, 'I knew it! I knew she would not serve the fresh fish. She is a glutton. She could only eat food in this house. While her mates are now having two or three kids running around their homes, here we are, yet without any child, except food and other luxuries. How do you expect me to go to barbeque spot at this hour of the day simply because your bossy wife refused to give me part of my benefits as your mother? Let her keep her fish, I am not hungry!'

I did not need my husband to come back to tell me what happened, because I heard everything. He tried to convince his mother about his wrong assumption, but to no avail.

After this very incident, it was hell living in my home. The siblings would come already prepared for war, even when I tried as much as I could to accommodate. Also, his mother would come with the threat of bringing another wife for him, and all manners of pressures. I became so fervent in prayers, but the more I tried to adapt, the farther my husband was moving towards the side of his family.

Traveling home to his parents became rampart, and any attempt to challenge his constant lonely visitations always ended in violence. At a point, he was completely separated from me. He moved to the visitor's room; we stopped praying together, eating together ceased, and many joint activities were halted. I spent most of the nights crying for help. Nothing came up from him. Before I knew it, I began losing weight at a stage of becoming so obvious that a colleague at work talked to me about it.

The courage I gathered from friends and colleagues gave me the strength that sustained me until this date. Thank God for Catherine, who shared her experience on the same issue. She told me how she stood on her feet to drive all her in-laws away from her home. Before her advice, I could not stand in front of my husband to insult him, but Catherine taught me how to fight against the bully. Since then, I think, some respect was accorded to me in my house (smile). It has been so violent and uneasy ever since, but it is what it is.

I know you do not want to see my back, it's full of scars inflicted by my husband. He became so brutal. The man I married is now always aggressive. I can't remember the last time he ate my food, and we stopped going out together."

The way Mrs. Lawson became emotional forced Mr. & Mrs. Benson to cut in. They both echoed, "That's alright. Now we have got to know the origin of that problem. With God, everything should be alright." She was offered a glass of water and asked if she would like some snacks. She nodded positively and was served.

CHAPTER 5
The Root

Mrs. Lawson's hearty reports touched her hosts, although it was never believed that her husband could not have his own story to tell, hence the promise to invite her husband in that regard so they could mend the broken relationship. Mrs. Benson showed her concern and sympathized with her friend for all she had gone through in her marriage, especially on the loss of their first pregnancy and the inability to conceive since then.

After they saw Mrs. Lawson off, the couple viewed all what was said by Mrs. Lawson, and some faults were dished out from all sides. Ranging from the parents to the families, friends, colleagues at work, and to the affected parties, that is, Mr. & Mrs. Lawson. A journal was created on the family's behalf to highlight their differences, mistakes, faults, and shortcoming for onward reformation, which was envisaged to help the couple and many others who would find themselves in similar storm.

In all of what Mrs. Lawson said, **the following points highlighted:**

- Association vs Assimilation
- Impact of Parental Assistance in Forming Relationship
- Importance of Priesthood Assistance vs Prayer Support
- Family Interrelationship via Marriage
- Misplaced Priority
- One Change, Changes Everything
- Your Friend Will Either Make or Break You
- The Broken Gate

All the above, as highlighted by the Bensons, are the rising point to the diminishing point of a stormy marriage. Most often, people see them as norms, hence the idea of *there is no perfect marriage*, but when critically viewed, there are some marriages that hardly experience such turbulence because of their alertness to some of the above points.

Association versus Assimilation: In every relationship, association always facilitates assimilation. At one point in life, a man and his wife must have had a first contact notwithstanding where or how. The first impression establishes the lifetime experience and foundation of the marriage. For as many that meet at the club, or other social gatherings, it always controls their lifestyles, thereby causing confusion later in life where either of the party attempt a change of lifestyle. Very likely, the first appearance connects a man to a woman. It may be by her mode of dressing, how she comports herself in public or at the place of work, or it can even be at the place of worship.

It is therefore important to improve such attitude for better. Too many, once they got married, tend to withdraw some values under the pretense of child-bearing or mere carelessness. As a result, a man who loves seeing his wife ever attractive will begin to lose interest in such a woman. This simply means both the man and woman should maintain the qualities they possess at the onset of their relationship.

The worst is when a woman pretended to be submissive at the beginning and switches to her real nagging type shortly after being wedded, this always disconnect affection. It is either the one opting out seeing his or her partner as a bad one, or the other looking at his or her partner as inferior or lower than standard. Hence, most men taking another wife after years of getting married.

In the case of the Lawsons, they met at a Christian program as youths with the same faith, although this could not rule out violence due to some cracks on their wall.

***Impact of Parental Assistance in forming a relationship*:** Parents may not be involved in casual relationships, but it is imperative to seek for parental assistance and advice at the onset of a serious relationship. This is because the journey that is about to commence in a child's life is always a trip already ended by parents. There are some mysteries that may be hidden to a child which does not require special eyes for the parents to unlock. More so, the lasting solution to some problems originates before the evolvement of such problems, these are always handy at parents' disposal.

Some will argue, "What if the parents are dead?" As a matter of fact, it is irrelevant if the parents are alive or not. There are cases of orphans who had never sighted their parents in life, yet they fulfill destiny. That is, there will always be someone who has been performing the parental roles in the past. They also qualify to be part of the marital journey.

Many marriages suffer today because parents were side-tracked out of love. Even where the parents were involved, some of their advice is often outdated in the sight of their wards, hence, the problems that remain unsolved.

In the report given by Mrs. Lawson, they both involved their parents at some point before their wedding. This was established in Mrs. Lawson and her mother seeing the Pastor for the dreams, and the marriage interview and counseling on the side of Mr. Lawson. When it happens that way, and problems are still emerging in such marriage, one would think God is absent in the home. Directly and indirectly, God is not an author of confusion, it's either He is not in the marriage fully or has not been there at all. The bedrock of every marriage should be God. When all obedience is duly observed, He will direct the affairs of the home. It requires the fear of the Lord, which endows wisdom in its ramifications.

Importance of Priesthood Assistance versus Prayer Supports: It is very essential to involve God at the beginning of a serious relationship that's meant for marriage. The Priesthood directives and prayer supports are always the foundational pillars that sustain marriages in the face of adversity. God will not change His words, what He says, He will surely do. Involving God via His vessels avails the opportunity of seeing dangers before it has been launched. Although some believe hearing from God it is not real, He still speaks.

This was established when the relationship between the Lawsons would commence. It was recorded that Mrs. Lawsons had several dreams in conjunction with the *association versus assimilation* they both initiated at the camp as team workers throughout the course of their staying together at the kitchen. It has been destined that the two would be team player for the rest of their lives. When she narrated the dreams to her mother, she took the right steps by contacting the Pastor, who supported them spiritually. No wonder there was a good family that took their time to restore the marriage.

Family Interrelationship via Marriage: Society is what it is today in size, demography, culturally, and politically as a result of the *interaction and interrelationship* that is coexisting in diversity. When a boy child brings into his family a girl child from another family, the families become one instantly. Love has no boundary. In the story of Mrs. Lawson, her visits to her husband's family introduced her first, then the introduction led to an expansion of familiarity. No matter the size of a family, either large or small, an addition is made the moment a boy child finds his best half.

Humans are full of differences, nonetheless, adaptation and tolerance always cover a multitude of weaknesses where they are wisely applied. In some families, the in-laws are often more cordial to each other than their wards who actually joined them together. Hence, the happy homes we see in our society. Some issues therefore would be settled to the root completely if parents play their roles in the lives of their wards.

Misplaced Priority: Among the points that surfaced from Mrs. Lawson's story was the issue of *misplaced priority*. Most times, couples are so attached to extended family responsibilities at the expense of theirs. Once a man and a woman officially bond together as a couple, the priority should be about their well-being. These includes financial, material, spiritual, and social. One would think that the first fruit of the Lawsons could have been the pregnancy lost during the wedding ceremony of a cousin who could as well be avoided with passion. Anyone could blame Mr. Lawson for going with his wife for the occasion, in spite of the state of her condition. But, to an extent, it was normal because what God had join-together let no pregnancy put them asunder, hence the irreplaceable loss.

Unfortunately, the journey they believed shouldn't be embarked alone became a journey the husband took without his wife, after a series of marital havocs had been caused. Some men would ignore the children's school fees to sponsor an extended family members' problem. It is good to help others, but it should be within the budget size of the family. The mind should be robbed together before involving in any external responsibility.

Where there is a good dialogue, responsibilities will be taken up both internally and externally without causing any problem. But where there is no cooperation via understanding, the home will always shake at the instance of responsibilities. Two heads are better than one, that is where prudence lies.

One Change, Changes Everything: It takes only one fight to create a gap between the couple. If there is any couple who stands for life, it is the couple who knows the hotspot of their family disagreement. No matter how dearie a couple can be, there are some differences either by culture, norms, or traditions that make one to differ from the other. At some points, these differences tend to cause confusion which will involve the application of maturity, forgiveness, understanding, and tolerance. At this hotspot, only the couple can genuinely subdue or suppress the effect on the family.

Sometimes, inability to do so may cause a damaging change. Once there is a damaging change, the sweetness in that marriage is gradually leaving. For a couple who enjoy sleeping in one room, on the same bed, a night of sleeping separately may be the damaging change. Obviously, it will affect praying together, having breakfast, lunch, and dinner together. This will usher in making friends outside the home, it may also involve taking counsel from outsiders. Things may begin to fall apart therein, and center may never be able to hold it forever. Your spouse is your best friend, there is no perfect covering apart the shared covers.

Your Friend Will Either Make or Break You: In the case of Mrs. Lawson, the result of seeking counsel from an outsider constituted a lot to her troubled home. As a matter of fact, no one can give more than what he/she possesses. Her friend's method of solving domestic problems was invoked into her life, but because men are not the same. Men are equally born, but not equally bred. Instead, for her to experience peace and love in her home, it was all chaos. It may be either man or woman, it is highly imperative to watch the effects of some of the friends on the family affairs.

Again, it is important to associate with friends who can add positive values to the home. A drunkard will always influence his friend in a matter of time, and an irresponsible woman will gradually turn a virtuous woman around as they keep bonding. It is better to remain unmarried than to be married to someone who cannot be your friend.

Unknown to many, especially women, some of the so-called friends mislead their friends to derail them on marital journey just out of jealousy. They seldom claim to reject some insults and maltreatment from their own husbands, whereas they are next to nothing in their homes. It is always the case where levels are not the same, but the ignorant ones stoop so low to associate with them. Some complaints of many women are the norms in another family, but how can it be discovered when they are not living together. Therefore, it is essential to look before leaping. Prayer remains the only friend in the face of marital adversities.

The Broken Gate: Disagreement between the husband and wife leaves their home with a *broken gate*. It is like a soup without salt. This often avails the opportunity for the intruders to penetrate. In fact, it is the arena of wasteful lifestyle. For any home to progress, it takes the full support and cooperation of the couple. The Bible says about the virtuous woman, "*She sees a field and buy it…*" Proverb 31:16.

The difference between a house and home

is the foundation and the management. Once a couple share the same dream of peace and harmony, the size of the abode is irrelevant, they are bound to making a habitable home. Whereas a couple on two parallel lines can never see the same vision or share the same dream.

The family may become the dictators and directors in a home with the *broken gate*. That is when the mother-in-law has to tell her daughter or son what to do and how to do it in their own matrimonial home. To live a good life, breed responsible children, and enjoy a good relationship in marriage, the gate must remain unbroken.

Mr. Benson insisted that he had to hear from his friend before concluding on who was the troubleshooter. He further said that he had lived with so many couples in his lifetime, and could tell that there are different attitudes, and reasons why some couples seem incompatible. He teased his wife about how he had been applying maturity to ensure stability in their family. Mrs. Benson also responded by saying she had been so tolerant with her husband too, since it takes two to tango. Nothing is as good as a good home.

When talking about friends who add values to good lifestyle, Mr. & Mrs. Benson can be reckoned with. They stood the gap to bridge and mend it, both physically and spiritually. They are well respected and honored in their community. So many marriages need genuine interventionists this day to safeguard the interest of a better tomorrow for our society in general.

Whenever the need arises, it is part of humanity to invest in the smooth running of homes. Observe a hotspot, crease a possible awareness to the affected couple together, do not call one to complain about the other, else, an unending problem may arise, one may live his/her entire life carrying the guilt for the cause of a broken relationship. Be a homemaker, not a home breaker.

NOT WITHOUT FLAWS

CHAPTER 6
The Unintended Compromise

It took the Bensons a whole week to contact Mr. Lawson for his own part of the story, and for a permanent solution to the problem. This time, there was no fear of rude interference from his wife. He came on a beautiful Saturday with a high spirit. Although what Mrs. Lawson told their family friends was enough to judge Mr. Lawson and concluded that he was responsible for the problem in the family, he was given an avenue to defend himself.

As usual, Mr. Benson ordered for a palatable cuisine from his wife for his friend, which was made ready before Mr. Lawson arrived. He was led straight to the table. Joyfully they all partook on the table. After a while, the discussion commenced. This time, the meeting was like a defendant before the jury, because the couple told him they had enough questionnaire for him to defend. He laughed and indicated his readiness for the task.

It was not at all like a confrontation, rather it was pre-planned to compare and contrast his own explanation and the additional facts he had on the seed of discord in his family. He began by thanking his family friend and apologized for the show of shame he and his wife performed the last time he was invited. He further thanked them for the patience they had in addressing their issues. He confirmed that he had observed little changes in the life of his wife within the few days.

He turned to his childhood friend, Mr. Benson, and said, "My friend, you know me very well and the story behind my marital cord with Janet is not full without mentioning your name. I love my wife whole heartedly, she was the best choice I made that day when I asked for her hand in marriage, but her sudden changes in character remained a mystery to me, as a matter of honesty.

I did all I was asked to do, both spiritually, morally, emotionally, and financially, during our courtship, engagement, and wedding. I became a member of her family and she did the same with us in my own family. We never had any reason to disagree on decisions, and whatever comes first from any of us is what we must do. This privilege was abused by my wife shortly after our wedding. My wife will not inform me ahead of bringing his families to the house to ask for money. In fact, she would have concluded on how much money to be given with the person before presenting it to me, and most times in the presence of the beneficiary.

This uncared attitude on several occasions put us in debts. Many times, we skip our house rent and some other expenses to recover from the unbudgeted responsibilities. I remember a day when one of her friends came with fabric materials. The lady said the materials were for another friend's birthday. This fabric was scheduled as uniform for all friends and their families. That time, my wife was still struggling to pay her school fees at the school, so I was jubilating inside of me that she had a good reason to reject the materials. Instead, she took for both of us. I excused them at the living room to the study, out of annoyance. To worsen the case, my wife brought the friend to where I was to plead for the purchase of the clothe. In order to the avoid public disgrace, I concurred. After the party, we suffered for about two months to get over the irrelevant expenditures.

The major problem began after she lost her first pregnancy. She accused me and my family for having part in the sad incident. Truly, I took her home based on my mother's instruction. She was not aware, because it was difficult for me to relay the message to her based on our religious belief. One afternoon, I received a call from my wife at work in which she told me there was breaking news. I was put in suspense for some hours.

After the terrible traffic, I got home in fear and anxiety to know what the news was. She told me to relax and freshen up first, still been inquisitive about the news, she became dramatic about it; she told me to eat first, my tension decline when I observed that the news was not going to be heartbreaking. She eventually handed over an envelope to me. When I opened it, I saw the heading of our family hospital and recollected she went for a medical checkup few days back, I could not understand the content. She explained to me that she was positive on the pregnancy test. I was extremely excited to know that in a few months, I would hold my first fruit.

I could not wait to share the good news with my mother, who was my gist partner before I got married. She was happy to hear the good news and she prayed for sustainable strength for the mother-to-be. At the conclusion of our conversation, she told me that in my family, women with their first pregnancy are specially celebrated at the end of the first trimester. That the celebration would involve the older women of the family and must be done in my father's house.

Initially I declined, because giving her our religious belief, which was contrary to such traditions. She told me it would not have any effect on our belief. I bottled this information for weeks because I knew my wife would turn it down vehemently. On the other hand, because we were both new in child-bearing processes, I knew we would still rely on her experiences to succeed in safe delivery, so I obliged.

There was a wedding ceremony of one of my cousins coming up towards my wife's first trimester, so I decided to seize the opportunity for her own celebration. On the day we arrived, my father ordered my siblings to kill one of the biggest goats he had, there were enough food to entertain all the extended family members who came to greet us, especially those who could not attend our wedding. Little did I know that was the celebration my mother told me.

In the morning, while some relatives were going up and down for the real wedding of my cousin, I asked my mother about the celebration she told me, and she said, 'Oh there is no special celebration than what was done the previous night; all it required was to prepare food in respect of the expectant mother for people to eat.' That was all about the celebration.

We both participated fully in the wedding ceremony; my wife put all her efforts in supporting other women in the day's activities from morning till the evening when everyone dispersed from the reception hall. We were all tired and slept like logs of woods. Somehow in the middle of the night, my wife woke me up with a complaint of an excruciating pain on her back, I knew it was as a result of going from pillar to pole to ensure the success of the wedding. So, I told her to go for another cold bath. She did, but it was not effective. She became more restless and groaning in pain. I could not sleep again, so we then went into prayer. At the time when she could not bear the pain any longer, she suggested taking a pain killer she had in her bag.

I agreed because I wanted anything that would relief her pain. The condition became normal until suddenly she screamed, 'Jesus!'

I quickly ran to her. What I saw was her

crying like a baby, she was bleeding. The monthly circle came back. I checked the time; it was 3 o'clock in the morning, a thought of going to the hospital came to my mind, but there was no hospital nearby. I was seriously praying for the day to break so we can take off and return to the city for a proper medical attention. The blood flow was consistent, my wife was crying profusely, I personally didn't want my parents to know what was going on.

Immediately the clock stopped on 5 a.m. and we packed all our bags to the car, bid the families farewell, and left for our station. It was a one-hour drive to the town. I went straight to the hospital to get a medical support for my bleeding wife. She was admitted and attended to in my presence.

Dr. Akins broke the sad news to me on Tuesday morning that we lost the pregnancy. I was pained to the bones, but summoned courage to avoid my wife's negative reactions to her lost. I promised to support her in domestic activities pending the time she recovered. Dr. Akins blamed us for risking the early pregnancy for events that were not too compulsory to attend, although I knew the secret behind the inevitability of the journey. He promised that within a short while, she would be pregnant again.

What was expected to happen within a few months took several years to occur. By its virtue, my wife became a terror in our domain. I tried all my possible best to assure her that we were in it together, all to no avail. My mother later knew about the incident. She blamed herself for enforcing the family traditions on us, especially since we didn't believe in its effectiveness. Be it as it might, all my family supported and loved her, but it was like she closed her heart from every one of them.

At a juncture, all my siblings stopped coming to us, and any time they were forced to come, it was always a hell in the house. I became separated from my family. My mother could not stop coming to me, so my wife saw it as a rude intervention to our privacy. No friend, except the two of you who live around us, could come to our home again.

I love my family; I am the eldest of the four children, my father could not do anything without my consent and my siblings' progress depends on my moral and financial supports, so I had no excuse to let them down, but I had been on parallel lines with my wife because of her unnecessary anger towards them. Dating and relationship covers a lot of differences that can only come out later in the marital journey of life as couples grow together after wedlock.

I could not have imagined my wife's recent attitude from the first day we met at the camp. She may claim that life challenges caused her to change, but I will still believe she was hiding her real identity just to get hold of me. I am not saying I regretted my choice among all the beautiful ladies at the camp that day, but honestly, I didn't know I was in for a serious mess like this. Janet was such a reserved and hardworking girl, so brilliant and devoted, those traits actually fascinated me to her.

When I told my parent about Janet, they strongly opposed our relationship because she was not from the same town as me. They told me it was their expectation that I would marry a lady from our town. According to them, it will avail the opportunity of background discoveries, and strengthen mutual understanding of our norms. As fate would have it, I have never dated any girl from my town. I told them anything without a remedy should be treated without relevance, as a result, they were without any option. However, they accepted her and treated her as if she was a native. I ensure my mother held her closer to herself so she could be lectured about our customs and norms.

Everything became normal, as expected, before the unending enmity. She hated my mother like a beast, and she has no favorite among my siblings as well. There is no more peace in the house, especially since Timmie came to live with us. I am strongly confused."

Mr. and Mrs. Benson were so attentive to the out-pour of their friend, but the silence was broken when Mr. Lawson mentioned Timmie. "Who is Timmie, and who is he to you? asked Mr. Benson."

Mr. Lawson was a bit reluctant in response to the question. He told them frankly that Timmie was his first son from another woman. He further said that he was forced to accept his mother's idea of having a second wife out of wedlock because of his wife's attitude. Timmie was born three years after his marriage with Janet, though not known to her till date.

Mr. Benson, pressing further, asked, "Where is Timmie's mother?"

Mr. Lawson was quick to respond this time. He said Timmie's mother re-married to another man after two years of not getting full attention from him because of his legal wife. Timmie was raised by his grandmother before he came to join them few years ago.

The story of the Lawsons was so pathetic, especially the loss of their first pregnancy that caused the wife to be barren. Mr. Benson consoled his friend and promised to support him in restoring peace to their home. Prayer was led by Mrs. Benson for the families, their careers, and their entire heart's desires. Mr. Lawson spent almost the whole day with his friends and was fully restored emotionally about life in general. At the end of their discussions on general issues that concerned the nation, as in politics, sports, and business, Mr. Benson said to his friend, Mr. Lawson, "Something came to my mind just now."

In response, his friend asked, "What could that be?"

Mr. Benson said, "I think we need a professional intervention on this matter?"

Mr. Lawson was confused about what that really meant, so he pressed further for explanation. Mr. Benson said it was a marriage counseling therapy that had really helped marital restoration. He assured his friend that these professionals would not only restore peace and tranquility, but they would also train the couple on how to handle life challenges for better interactions in their home.

"That sounds good," was Mr. Lawson's response.

The whole day was a success as Mr. Lawson returned home so lighted in spirit. As usual, after the departure of Mr. Lawson, the couple, Mr. & Mrs. Benson reclined in their living room to highlight some points that came up in their visitor's story. Some were similar to what the wife said before, some were contrary, and some came up as weaknesses on the part of the husband. However, it was discovered that Mr. Lawson's inability to differentiate what he could and could not do after becoming a married man constituted to the storm in his home.

The points were highlighted as follows:

- Too Much Attachment to Family After Marriage
- Inability to Set and Establish Rules in the Marriage
- Dangers of Dishonesty

- The Tiny Crack on The Wall
- Sour Love/Bitter Love
- Irreparable Dent

Too Much Attachment to Family After Marriage: Apart from when a relationship is emerging to a stage of marriage, couples should learn how to create their own world. Running the affairs of the home should only involve God, and sometimes advice from the parents. Also, when considering advice, both the husband and wife should table the advice before each other to finally choose which one to apply, and how it will add value to their ideas.

Sometimes, many immediate family members offer advice that will suit their ulterior motives in gaining access to the affairs of a peaceful home. Ignorantly, a man or woman will take to such advice, and end up ruining his/her home. It is good to apply other people's ideas to whatever one is about to dangle into, but it is necessary to view such ideas in all perspectives which includes, considering one's status both in terms of finance, class, education, and family background. At times, what is good for the goose may be good for the ganders. Some priorities are not often set equally because of availability and capability. Unfortunately, some married couples make the mistakes of comparing themselves with classmates, neighbors, and colleagues.

In some part of the world, people believe that a newly married couple is an extension of the family ties, thereby, they always want to transport the norms in the old family to the new one. This often causes a lot of havoc, because in that new family, a stranger from another source had joined them with her own traditional background bound to be totally different from theirs. Many a time, in-laws view their daughter or sister in-laws as hostile, unwelcoming, rude, and lots more, of which can be regarded as character assassination because the characteristics given are never applied to them. It's just a mere cultural difference.

In a nutshell, once a couple glues together, there must be a boundary of interference for the couple to live and enjoy marriage. Mr. Lawson did not detach himself from his parent quick enough, despite his education and religious advancement from the faith of his parents, of which still believes in traditional rituals. Example was the pregnancy celebration that ended up destroying their first ever pregnancy. Family should be one love and one faith.

Inability to Set and Establish Rules in The Marriage: Another important weakness in the home of the Lawsons is their inability to set rules and standard. For a home to succeed without unnecessary stress and debt, it is paramount to have one voice on planning and expenditures. No one should involve on unimportant spending. Monthly budget must be put in place, which may either lead to transferring left-over capital to the next month, spend it as excess on luxuries, or save it for future investment.

As a matter of fact, every woman loves to be a golden fish everywhere, but that should be done at a maximum convenience. Human and woman wants are insatiable. By virtue of that, to check the spirit of excessive materialistic buying, rules must be put in place, and strictly established. None of the couple must affect the wellbeing of the home because of any external evitable responsibilities.

Most of the failed marriages nowadays came up as consequences of lack of cooperation. In fact, most women, or even including some men, are so unruly when it comes to setting priorities. This is because most people cannot differentiate between wants and needs. Where needs are utmost most important, wants can be optional.

Howbeit, inability to tackle the most pressing needs within the available resources many times creates some form of disagreement in homes. Where this occurs, only the wise spouse sees the implication of focusing on wants rather than the necessities and always guides against its future side effects. A woman will always want to pay off the children school fees before attending to any extended family responsibilities, but the man would never want any disgrace from his families, thereby, he will find a way of postponing his own immediate family's need until later. Yes, it is good to assist others, but not to the level of your own family suffering, except if the postponement cannot cause any harm. This is not limited to helping others, it may even be for unnecessary pleasure and luxuries.

Dangers of Dishonesty: Mr. Lawson could have saved his wife's health and the life of the unborn child if per adventure he disclosed his mother's order on the pregnancy celebration.

Two heads are better than one, hence the purpose of being married. Dishonesty may seem to be a shortcut to winning the heart of one's heart, or agreement to carry out some ideas. Many husbands will lure their wives into investments that are not real, which at the end may cause a substantially huge loss. Thank God

Mrs. Lawson made it to the hospital, think of many other women who had lost their lives, simply because they were exposed to dangers from their husbands out of dishonesty.

Furthermore, Timmie was brought to their house as a cousin when he's actually the first son of Mr. Lawson. In many marriages today, men often bring their girl-friends home as family members and out of wickedness and jealousy, either the wives or children are attacked physically and spiritually. For a man to live happily, he must be honest with his wife. Most times, women don't believe their husbands' financial declaration, especially those who lack the importance of honesty.

Imagine a man who hides some money in his pocket, while deceiving the wife that he has none. If such a wife is a virtuous woman who loves to keep his family clean ventures to wash her husband's clothes now discovers such money, one would expect her to deliver the money to her husband, obviously; but it takes a woman of integrity to do so and ever trust the man again.

It's two ways though, as important as it is for the man to be honest, so is it significant for the woman to be trustworthy. It takes only one attempt to lose one's integrity. When a woman is not trustworthy, it will not only affect her husband, it will also affect her children. Children learn the deeds more than the sayings. These two virtues are enough to breed Godly children that our society needs at a time like this. Charity begins at home.

The Tiny Crack on The Wall: Right from the wedding reception, which marks the line of separation from other external forces, families, and friends' closeness, a couple should watch out for possible little cracks on their marital walls. It starts with phone calls and messages. Any phone calls that warrant leaving where your spouse is to answer will cause a crack. When there is a crack on the wall, so many living things can crawl and hide therein. Fake friends and wicked families are the creatures that love to hide withing the crack.

Fortifying the marital walls is a joint task that must be done. Where there is an inseparable association between husband and wife, no devil will instigate any of them against each other. The devil loves where there is no cooperation and oneness. Parents in-law are led to love their wards equally when they find out that whatever you say to one is said to all. Remember, as you lay your bed, so you'll lie on it. Only prayer and commitment to the things of God can really fortify the marital wall. Psalm 33:18.

Sour Love/Bitter Love: Every marriage starts with sweet love, but when the unexpected begins to happen, the sweetness disappears. When the effects are discovered earlier enough, many havocs may not be caused, but where ignorance exists, it's always too late to discover and recovered. That is why it is important to do a marital check up every time.

Funny as it may be, at times, journal of love lives

is necessary to garnish one's love life. How many times do you hear your spouse saying *I love you* in a day before and after the wedding? Shortly after your first baby, do you notice a reduction or increment of that gesture? This should be an equal expression, *it takes two to tango*.

Some women often transfer the love of their husbands to the children, and so do some men. Love is a lifetime commitment that should not interfere with anything. Just remember that you had once left your parents to join your husband or wife, leaving your parents to themselves. Any mistake of letting off the sweetness of marriage always lead to sour love.

Sour love leads to seeking alternatives elsewhere. A step outside the wedlock, either by choice or by influence, is always resulting in bitter love, especially for men. Sometimes, out of frustration, infatuating love becomes the only alternative as a means of avoidance. This may seem to give a temporary happiness. Like an alcoholic, the pleasure of having someone outside the marriage can be more expensive and a form of wasteful lifestyle. Some of the girls/women on such missions are looking for how to keep their souls and bodies together. They don't need to plan the future with any men; they have nothing to lose even if the table turns for their conditional lovers. Worthy of saying, too, is that many married women also engage themselves in extra-marital affairs under the guise of seeking for happiness.

The craziest thing any man or woman can do in a marriage is to seek extra marital alternatives. While the extra woman or man enjoy the regular quickie affairs, the lovers will still go back into their home to face the battles therein. Mr. Lawson was influenced by his mother to take another wife. The result was Timmie, who was living with them like an extended family member. Today some legitimate children are under the bondage of living as secondhand children in their homes due to *sour/bitter love*. Secret affairs may remain secret until the man gives up the ghost. Think of the many women and children who have been exposed to the insult of doing DNA testing to ascertain their relationship with their late fathers, simply because their parent got them in secrecy.

Irreparable Dent: A scar can never blend the skin, even if it is a graft. Have you ever asked why your wedding ring has no end? Marriage is fashioned to be unending, just like the ring, but when the unexpected begins to happen, the ring will immediately begin to open. When this occurs, dirt, rust, and discoloration will be inevitable. That is exactly what a sweet home may experience after the first misunderstanding. Although it is not possible for two people from different background to be in agreement at all times, but when the misunderstanding escalates to fight, that is where disconnection commences, and it becomes a dent in a beautiful relationship.

At the junction of conflicts, the devil is given the opportunity to showcase the ugly side and structures of the couple. That is when a man will have a negative critical look at the woman he once cherished and adored. Likewise, the woman will see the worst part of her husband's body. Meanwhile, it takes that one moment to see the partner in and out in a negative and annoying state. That is why after a series of incidents, a man especially begins to look at another woman lustfully.

Then comes the moments of appreciating the colleagues at work, who knows how to do best what his wife at home could not do, ranging from knowing how to dress, greet, smile, or even cook. On the other hand, only a few women disconnect quickly from the first affection they had for their husbands. No matter how much the man hurts, a woman will always want the storm to end. Hence the word, enduring marriage.

The dent is not limited to affecting only the couple where there are children. This is simply because, once the couple fails to settle their differences over night, the first thing that will happen will begin from their altar of prayer. In a home where morning prayer is a must before going out, a couple who is still having unresolved issues will never kneel down together to pray, especially where the woman feels she had been offended and was expecting a word of apology from her man, she may be giving attitudes just to show how bad she is feeling.

Honestly, it takes a man of valor to apologize for his fault, especially in some parts of Africa. Because of the background setting, men are ordained to use attack for defense. In spite of that, wisdom is required for a woman to take the first step to tender an apology. Many unexpected treats, gifts, and encouragement are part of the bundles reserved for such a woman who ignores claiming her right when there is a fight.

On the contrary, a woman who believe in equal rights and equal reactions may ignorantly tamper with the father-child relationship in her home. As we all know, women have an unusual closeness with children at home. Once the children notice the little discord between their parents, which shows a clear avoidance, they will bond more with their mother to pacify her. In this process, children, especially the male, may become so angry with their father that he may often be seen as a bully because they believe the food basket must be handled with care. In the same vein, the father will feel bad that his children are going against him in his own house.

In short, unresolved issues can grow from mild to severe if a check is not put as soon as possible. To some extent, it causes emotional imbalances in the lives of every member of a home. An unhappy father will prefer to be by himself even if he is in doer, and as a matter of fact, there is limitation to how long a man or woman can keep to him or herself without flowing down to the children. Such children will lack human relations outside their homes.

Apart from the domestic effects, an unhappy couple will transfer their aggression to the workplace. To worsen it all, a subordinate officer may end up losing his or her job, as a result of emotional imbalance. For instance, an accounting officer who has a lot of errors in his or her transactions may be asked to stay away from the company's financial activities until he or she is psychologically alright. In a case where such a loophole cannot be afforded, this may be the end of such a job. This can even be a boss or supervisor. Once the emotional status has been tampered with, it will affect the positive discharge of duties and may also affect both the workers, the administration, and the clients.

Another major effect of unresolved fights or domestic disorder is how it affects the parent in-laws. All other effects may be easily rectified, but the one that has to do with the families in one way or the other is always like a wildfire. This is because gossip of discord moves faster than imagined. Before you know it, the majority of those who had seen the good sides of the couple will quickly team up with any family member who claims to be a victim of domestic transferred aggression, because blood is thicker than water.

Today in what ended up in divorce is always starting from a little unresolved misunderstanding mixed with ego. Socialism and structural rearrangement had equated men and women in the labor market. As a matter of fact, some men preferred to see their wives going out to work while they stay at home performing domestic works and babysitting, simply because such women are making more money than them; in return, they make them take up the financial responsibilities. In such family settings, it takes the grace of God, and strong humility and submission for the women to respect and honor the husbands. That also is the hotspot of power tussle where the woman will be waiting for her husband to come unto his knees anytime he did something wrong.

In the traditional gender role, before the contemporary took over, women are always afraid to fight with their husbands, because they knew it could affect so many parts of their lives. As a result, they were quick to apologize even when they were not at fault, just to keep their homes and make their men happy.

So many lives are wasting due to marital stress, gender notwithstanding. Meaning longevity can be derived from having a happy home. In the western world, some men are dying earlier than destined due to frustration. Many cannot live up to the standard because of child support, and the idea of leaving the houses they labored to buy for their wives as necessity compels. Also, many women could still be enjoying the fruits of their labor, if it was not for the sudden death resulting from maltreatment and constant beating by their husbands. Considering all the above facts, one will realize that in marital disorderliness, men and women are not without flaws.

Having considered the reports of Mr. & Mrs. Lawson, and for many others in their shoes, it is important to adopt all means to help them in rebuilding their homes. Mr. & Mrs. Benson had always been friends in need for so many couples around them. They are enjoying a good home and loved their friends to enjoy theirs, too. Sometimes, friends and colleagues do ask them whether or not they ever had any misunderstanding or disagreement between each other. The answer was always, "Yes, but we don't always allow it to put us asunder."

As a matter of fact, only few couples of this century have similar experience in the homes, that is, having a peaceful home.

CHAPTER 7
Therapeutic Intervention

As equality of rights and innovation is advancing, home front is experiencing pressures in terms of submission and dedication to families. Competition between couples is waging war against good relationship and interaction. The insatiable wants and inevitable needs of individual or collective challenges have left no room for human relations. Husbands are no more shouldering the total care of their families, thereby leaving no rooms for control and complete power over their wives, contrary to the ancient power bestowed on men as the commanders of affairs over everyone in their domains. What we see today is shared responsibilities that allow everyone to be equal with anyone. This single inadequacy makes the system in general not without flaw.

By virtue of the confusion of power and interference of contemporary gender roles with the traditional roles, it became imperative for social scientists to derive some solutions to help families in society. Among the solutions is Marriage Counseling and Therapy. These moves address the psycho and social repair and reformation. Once the center is unable to hold on, things tend to fall apart. The effects of these solution units of the social science cannot be over-emphasized because it has and is still helping a number of couples to redirect their love lives to how it was long before the marital derailment.

Out of frustration and constant misunderstanding, many people had lost their psychological values, thereby becoming threats to society. Sometimes, many people allow aggression brought over from home to spill on co-workers out of frustration and emotional imbalance, resulting in their interactions with others outside their families to be without flaws.

In most cases, comparison and lack of contentment is the source of a problem in some homes. This often occurs where association influences the way of life, particularly when economic and social status are not the same. Any man or woman who fails to recognize and associate his or her class will always feel inferior and bounce back on the partner at home.

Fabio and Norela were happily married for five years before relocating to Rockbelt. In the neighborhood, there was a lady named Tonia. She forced herself on Norela as a friend. This was easy because she was a hairdresser, and Norela used to patronize her. After sometimes, they became so close and cordial. One day, Norela went to Tonia's saloon to fix her hair, and as usual, some gist ensued. Unknown to Norela, Tonia was envious of her and the happy home she was enjoying with her husband. She decided to get rid of her and expose her to a serious marital challenge.

Tonia knew Fabio, Norela's husband, as a

very hardworking man who could not stand his wife lacking any good thing, an attitude that was opposite in her own marriage, she got to know how they fared in their home because Norela always said her husband did this and that. Meanwhile, to carry out her prank and to spike a marital fire in her friend's house, Tonia lied that her husband just bought a plot of land on her behalf and that plan had completed on building the house within just six months. She advised Norela to pressure her husband to do the same thing for her instead of giving her stipends for material needs.

Ignorantly, Norela started her crazy attitude of fighting and nagging at home. This attitude had been noticed in her for a while because Fabio knew she changed as a result of her closeness to her hairdresser. He tried to convince his wife, but it was falling on her deaf ear; so, he decided to keep in secret, some of his moves so the wife could not tell her friend.

A six-room duplex was recently purchased by Fabio with the intention of giving it as a surprise package to mark their wedding anniversary, of which Norela had no clue. Day by day the insult and disrespect continued, and he became a useless reckless spender who had no plan of building a house for his family. Fabio persevered, but he always notified his mother-in-law, who also tried her best to put her daughter in order, yet all was in vain. The house that was once peaceful began to experience commotion.

Despite the unreasonable attitudes of Norela, Fabio never stopped his plan to surprise his wife. He paid for a new car to accompany the new house, still without the knowledge of his wife. Two weeks to the anniversary, Tonia, the hairdresser, called Fabio during the office hours. It came as a surprise because it has never happened before; so, he thought there was an emergency at home. Instead, Tonia was calling to invite her friend's husband to a hotel for a private discussion. Fabio recorded her conversations for evidence, to be sure if what Tonia told his wife about the house her husband built for her was real.

He asked Tonia when they would be moving to the new house. He was shocked to hear that she was just teasing her friend all that while. He played the recorded conversation to his mother, and Norela's just for them to know the source of their problem, and to entrap the devil behind their downfall. The two mothers told him to suspend action until all of them would be around to intervene.

The date fixed for the parental intervention was on the wedding anniversary day. Unknowingly for both mothers, Fabio secretly furnished the house and got it ready for use. The celebration was not meant for any get-together because of the problems in the home, so nobody envisaged a party, but the event planners who had taken over for dinning and wining. A day before the meeting, Fabio sent the venue address to all the few friends he wanted for the occasion, including his mother and mother-in-law. He told them he wanted the intervention on a neutral ground outside his home. They both obliged and kept it a date.

On the morning of the anniversary, Norela's mother called and asked her to meet her at the address given by Fabio. She did not even know her husband would be there, too. It was a great surprise for all of them when they found themselves in a big new mansion, gorgeously furnished for their own family issue. It was still amazing to them until the Master of Ceremony in his welcome address told them they are in the house of Mr. Fabio and Mrs. Norela Hopewell. Norela could not believe her ears when her name was mentioned. No doubt, she knew the house was not too big for what her husband could possess, but she felt so bad that she knew nothing about it before that day.

Mr. Fabio's speech at the occasion left no room for any other intervention of both their parents, because he did not even want the issue of his wife's fake friend disrupt the good time. He said wrong association caused his wife to lose her value in the past, and that she had been totally forgiven. He concluded by saying, "Honey, this beautiful mansion made me a reckless spender." She hugged him and apologized. The party was declared opened with the tour of the beautiful mansion.

The story above was what Mr. Robertson told his visitors just to debunk that fact that only the family interference could cause confusion in a marriage. The Bensons presented their observations to the Therapist, who was also a friend to give him slight ideas of what went wrong in Lawson's family. He was happy that those highlights would make healing and reformations easy in helping the troubled marriage. He was happy, too, that the couple was still living together despite the tide of the storm. He scheduled them for a one-in-one meeting, that is, without the third party, the Bensons. Mr. Benson supported the idea, and they all dispersed.

Having gone through the highlights initiated by the Bensons, Dr. Robertson did not spend much time in finding the cause and effects of their weaknesses, rather he chose to apply practical treatment. He titled it *What I need to Do to Help My Flaws*. He told them there was no need to ask who caused what, but he would lead them to know what is expected from a wife and husband as well. He began with the woman.

From Her to Him:

- Sincerity
- Submission
- Respect
- Support
- Care
- Perseverance
- Prudency
- Sensitivity
- Contentment

Sincerity: This virtue among others is very essential at the onset of relationship. The luckiest person in the issue of marital life is the man or woman who received the same level of love and affection from the partner. Some marriages in this century are not based on genuine love. The fair of loneliness and greed for prosperity from some are the reasons behind fake relationships, and to be candid, it shows whenever there is little misunderstanding. Where there is genuine love and sincerity, it takes a short while for such couples to settle their problems, unlike where the marriage is falsely built and conditional. Most often, the insincerity is initiated by a partner willing to take advantage of the other, it can either be the man or woman, it depends on who has what to lose at the end.

Double dating either by man or woman can never create an avenue for till death do us part affairs in marriage. Just like gambling in most cases, a lady who engages in dating two men with a mindset of marrying the first to possess a car or attain a certain position, has set in an avenue to be tossed like the plant beside the riverbank. The first man to possess a car may soon be outdated when the other obtains the newest model. Out of regrets, she will be blaming herself for lack of patience. If per adventure the other one is still single, or irresponsible in his own home too, there may be a time when they will cross again. And before they know it, the old affairs may be reactivated.

Many stories like that have been heard, and as a result, the real husband at home will become irrelevant and valueless. But when the marriage is built on sincerity, the woman will be committed to her home in the thick and thin.

Submission: The major problem facing marriages nowadays is a power tussle. Now that there is no boundary on how far a woman can go academically, it is becoming so difficult for some women to switch attitudes from work to home. Especially the majority who are more professional than their husbands. This is because, being at the elms of affairs at work, many of them are superior officers to men older than their husbands and they tend to forget that the rank at work cannot leave their seats.

To really enjoy marriage, there must be psychological pointers to outrightly control the attitude at home and at work, even if it means being the bread winner of that home. The Bible also confirms this in the book of Ephesians 5:22. Apart from all the Holy books, there are plenty of numbers of traditions and customs all over the world support the full submission of the woman to her husband, if she really wants a peaceful marriage.

Respect: In marriage, contrary to the popular saying of 'respect is reciprocal,' reciprocating respect in marriage is not in fair measure; that is, no woman should respect her husband because she believes he must do that to her in return. Of course, the respected man will put such a woman at the center of his heart. The respect may not be when the wife kneels to greet him that he should prostrate too, but it will speak for such woman in her absence.

No man will be careless about a woman who gives him respect, he will go extra miles to always make her happy for making him valuable. Because such a man sees himself as a precious stone, he will not hesitate to crush any pain that wants to come near his jewel. Therefore, it is essential for a woman to respect her man.

Support: *No man is an island* is a popular phrase that encourages support. So be it the best supporter in life's journey is the partner in marriage. Any man having the full support of his wife is a high-flyer. Another common phrase says, behind a successful man, there is a woman. Having said all these, it becomes a debt for any woman who fails to support her husband. Very worthy to note, it may not be financially but morally. A man with the right-thinking faculty will generate and facilitate good business ideas that will in return be profitable to his family.

Support to one's man can also be monetary. A good wife will be open in all her financial incomes, this will avail the opportunity of building future assets in terms of business, mortgage, and other luxuries of life. An awesome dream may be killed by lack of support from the home front. So many times, people ask from some men why they are still struggling financially when they have rich wives, the answers are always showing they have no clues to their wives' financial status.

Training the children in the home need full support of the woman morally and financially. Paying school fees and other necessity should be a joint task, there are cases of homes where some women believe it is the sole responsibility their husbands to pay school fees and other necessities, as a result they make the work like clock and run from pillars to poles.

Above all, a praying wife is the life wire of her home. A praying wife is a like a hen that lays the golden eggs. These sets of women have special eyes, ears, and inexplainable wisdom. They perceive problems before striking. Many times, the challenges of some men in life occurred as results of not having a 'backbone.' Thank God for some men who are religious, most often, they are the shakers and movers of their weak wives, although their percentage is very small.

Invariably, a woman who thinks she has no money to support her husband financially must be able to finance him on her knees in prayer. When the fire of the family altar is greatly charged, both progressive and marital ideas will be flowing, and with time, the husband will be in the position to upgrade her business endeavors. The greatest expectation of a man from his wife is unwavering supports in all its ramifications.

Care: In the Bible, Proverbs 14 precisely, it was slated in full, the traits of a good wife as regards her husband, the children, and the entirety of the home. Care is very important, and its double edged. As a matter of fact, it is the second aspect of marital spice to ginger lifelong marital benefits. The quantity is always even, and it is not hidden when it exists. One should remember that both the husband and wife were once under the custody of their parents, where they enjoyed inestimable privileges, like a baby on his or her mother's back that is careless about the distance of the journey.

Such privileges are interrupted by a love bird who agreed to take up the care from the parents. That is to say, the man agrees to cater and pamper the woman just like her parents used to do, and vice versa. Therefore, maltreating the husband in terms of not feeding him well, not washing his clothes either personally, through laundry machines, or dry cleaning and by not giving good advice can make a woman irresponsible. This simply means such a woman may not be a caring mother to her children. When you see a good-looking husband, give the credit to his wife. Furthermore, a woman who cannot pray for her husband can never stand in the gap for her children.

A caring woman always customize her food directly and indirectly. If a man cannot dislike food prepared by someone else or does not detect some missing important spices in food outside, then his wife is not caring enough. This is not limited to the husband alone; likewise, many children will reject some food outside simply because it does not taste the same way with their mother's. Caring mothers make their family eat food like medicines rather than eating medicines like food.

Another important aspect of care is making provision for their personal house. Careless woman will not see anything wrong in living in a rented house for donkey years when there is provision and enough resources to erect one for the family. It takes deep care for a woman to bring up an idea for preparing for their old age. A caring woman can diagnose her husband's and children's fitness without any medical instrument. When a man is broke, it is always obvious for a good woman to know, but a careless woman will not mind the look or state of mind of her husband.

Very essential, every woman must be familiar with the bull and bear outlooks of her husband, in order to apply caution whenever the hard time hits the man. The majority of men are not always happy when they cannot provide necessities. Imagine a man who cannot afford his immediate needs being pressurized for unnecessary wants. You cannot claim you love a man you don't care for.

Perseverance: Rome, they say, was not built in a day. Until recently, when economic status is improving. In the past, most couples usually rent cars on their wedding days, except for a few who are from wealthy families. What matters is the foundation they are building on, that is the academic achievement which is believed to be the pipeline to greatness. Yet, it takes a little while after the knot tying for some couples to build wealth of their own. The gap between coming together and having resources to enjoy life is the most delicate season in marital life.

Sometimes, many couples derail along the line for lack of perseverance. Sad as it may sound, many women who had been in marriage for years having experienced the good times with their husbands, constitute the greatest numbers of people seeking for divorce, simply because the going gets tough for their husbands. Some will say, "For better to stay, for worst for leave."

Such women can never have a permanent home, because they jumped over to the richer man than their ex-husbands, and immediately when they notice any problem in their newly found man they leave again. And the truth is that only a few people enjoy their second marriages. After some years of marriage, some men, by virtue of bad influences, can develop a strange attitude. Especially those who are not religious or Godly in any ways; they can be womanizing or love to hang around with friends.

Certainly, it will not be a welcome idea for the wives, but with prayers God will intervene. Actually, it might be predestined for such men to learn life lessons in a very hard way. Only through perseverance can some glorious destinies be fulfilled.

Perseverance remains the only weapon that can be used to face the challenges of extended families in both ways. One must be sincere. Many marital challenges are orchestrated from the woman's family, but often attributed to the mother-in-law, sister-in-law problems. Nevertheless, once a woman focuses on either jumping or breaking the marital hurdles, her maximum perseverance gives strength in the face of such adversity. Without perseverance, some women will fail in mothering, especially when the children transit from baby to young adults. It may seem challenging at times, but giving in the best level, where there seems to be no way out, is greatly rewarding.

Prudency: This is a great virtue. It is one of the best ways of building fortune. When a woman is prudent, she will be in better control of resources that are available for proper provision of necessities. Such woman avoids with passion, excessive or unnecessary spending, which in returns avails the opportunity of investing or save money on assets. Prudency is not the act of depriving one's family of good a life, but it serves as a check and balance, and encourages wise spending.

There are some women who cannot

manage resources, it starts from maintaining daily needs to the tune of fairly dividing little available resources to meet all requirements with maximum satisfaction. If a woman lacks prudency, she can never be satisfied with anything the husband put down for maintaining their home. There are cases of some who will buy excessively and reserve some items while very essential ones are still lacking in the house. In return, they will blame their husbands for not providing for the needs of their families.

At times the problems facing many marriages are not external, but from within of which lack prudency and better management from the side of the woman in the house plays a vital role. It is the duty of the man to provide for the wellbeing of his family, but not his duty to monitor how well his wife distributes the resources to cover every area of necessities. Unfortunately, some women are holding managerial positions at their various places of work but cannot manage their homes. Proverb 31 speaks volume about the qualities of a prudent woman, for every woman to read all the time.

Sensitivity: When the combination is right, husband and wife breath the same way, and there are some signs and signals in the body mechanism that operates the same way and at the same time. That is, where there is sincere love, what happens to one happens to the other. In most cases, men are not always paying attention because of the heavy responsibilities and the thought of how to meet those responsibilities overwhelms them, and this often affects their sense of discernment. Therefore, since the bodies are now acting as one, the best help a woman can render is to pick up the leftover of the other partner, and this is by being sensitive to their environment.

Sensitivity and discernment ability of some women are often misinterpreted to a bad attitude, in the sense of wrongful conclusion that a woman does not like a family member or friend whose main intentions were to harm the family. Good women and responsible mothers are the angels of their worlds. Sometimes, men don't listen to their observation and advice, especially if it pertains to their immediate family members of childhood friends, it can even be mere neighbors.

However, it is most advisable that women should handle issues like that with wisdom. Praying and committing one's family to the hands of God settles every area that can constitute loopholes in the family without causing havocs, confusion, or misunderstanding. In sum, a women's sensitivity is essential.

Contentment: Contentment is not found in having everything but being satisfied with the little one available. When a woman is appreciative on little efforts of her husband, she is opening avenues for more. Many a time, men are forced to divert some benefits to outsiders since they know their wives will not appreciate them. Apart from the diversion, lack of contentment constitutes a lot of havocs to sound health. Too many expectations and the attitude of anticipating many things can affect the psychological well-being hence, the increasing rate of depression and untimely death of some women.

When contentment is embraced in all its ramifications, food, clothes, and other materials of daily living will appear more surplus than can be viewed. Sometimes, the cheapest clothes will look more gorgeous on someone than the most expensive on another, it is just about the state of mind. It is therefore expectant of a woman to be fulfilled in whatever the husband provides for her and pray for a breakthrough on his endeavors for more blessings. A woman who is never satisfied can't see anything good in whatever her husband is doing to support the home. Such women are the types that end up having extra-marital affairs or cheat on their husbands to satisfy their greed and covetousness. Also, they don't always save for the raining days, or plan for a better future.

CHAPTER 8
Therapeutic Intervention II

The meeting between Dr. Richardson and Mrs. Lawson extended past what was earlier planned, making it difficult for him to be attended to. However, Mr. Lawson was asked to come back the following week. Also, it was a tactic to know if all he told Mrs. Lawson was effective. It was already 7 p.m. before they arrived back home, because of the high road traffic. Things have been taking a new form in their relationship since when their family friends, the Bensons, intervened. They are now praying, eating, and going out together on some occasions. So, with the little counseling Mrs. Lawson received, she promised herself to follow every step to ensure the restoration of her home.

She quickly went to prepare dinner.

After dinner, Mrs. Lawson put on one of her best sleeping robes and went to her bedroom as usual. Just an hour later when Mr. Lawson reclined to sleep in his bedroom too, he felt the best to activate the smooth relationship that departed from his home is to have some words with his wife, especially to apologize for all their dramas in the past. Apologetically, Mrs. Lawson sought for a place in her husband's heart for forgiveness. They both went through the handout, consisting all what she is expected to do in keeping her marriage. Mr. Lawson said, "If these are your responsibilities, I am sure mine will double them because I am a man." They prayed together for the grace to carry on.

One week after their last appointment, as scheduled, Mr. & Mrs. Lawson headed towards the therapist office for the conclusion part of their treatment. This time it is for Mr. Lawson's turn to be addressed. Dr. Richardson started by telling him how much he had prepared his wife for a better result at home, and he assured him that once he, Mr. Lawson, follows the steps highlighted on the handout meant for him, the home will experience inexplainable peace again.

To begin with, Mr. Lawson, did you notice any improvement in your wife? He answered positively that they are now so peaceful and cordial.

From Him to Her:

- Affection
- Openness
- Attention
- Reliable
- Caring

Affection: The first thing that motivates a lady to loving a man is the level of affection shown to her at the onset of the relationship. And sincerely, when a man loves a lady, he can call such a lady more than ten times in a day. He will put her picture at the center of his heart, willing to be by her side at all times. It is therefore imperative to keep that attitude for a lifetime in order to enjoy a happy home. Unfortunately, few months or years after the wedding, the fire of such affection becomes low by virtue of some other life challenges or commitment to work or business. As a result, the woman too will gradually get used to the random cordial interaction by substituting for other means of getting pleasure. This may be by spending much time on social media to make herself happy when the husband is not around.

This unnoticed menace creates a wide gap between couples. Some husbands don't remember to call their wives throughout the day while at the office to check on them, nor do the women in most homes; that means, once everyone disperses from home in the morning, they don't care about their partners till they return at night. It is the duty of a man to always check back on wives and children, whether they are in the same town or in different locations. By doing this, the hearts beat together, and the love wall is solidified. Some women get disappointed so quickly when they discover that the same men who had never given him breathing spaces in courtship, the men who always call and take them out are no longer doing the same in later years. So, to sustain and maintain a good home, the husband must be more affectionate.

Openness: The greatest harm a man can do to himself is failure to be opened to his wife. Some people believed that must not be allowed to know the total money her husband possesses, to some extent, the ideology is wrong. At the point of joining the groom and bridegroom, it has always been telling them that they are becoming one, therefore trying to hide the complete truth to one's partner is never an act of being smart, but foolishness and mayhem.

A man must carry his wife along in his financial dealings and be opened as well. When a man brings out money from a wallet, it is the general attitude of all women that the man has more to offer than he gives. Thereby, a genuine appreciation is withheld. But when the man openly gives what he decides to give without hiding anything, at times good women will suggest taking back some of the money, especially when she knows there is another area that needs financing.

This is a century where a man will invest in a business without the wife's knowledge, and when there is any eventuality against the success of the business, the first witness which supposed to be the wife won't be able to bear witness. There are cases of houses or other properties that have been unlawfully claimed from some men, simply because people knew those men are secretive about them. The worst are the men who died and left their children born outside wedlock to suffer in the background with identity denials. Once bitten twice shy, openness is the virtue that stands in absentia, it is very essential.

Attention: The very difficult crack on the wall of marriage that can never be easily covered is the lack of attention from a man. Of course, man must work, but it is necessary and significant to always create time for one's family. It depends on the schedule of the individual though, but be it as it may, spending enough time with the family will avail the opportunity for the man to know how his family fares.

Money is not everything, it is paramount to know where exactly one is dumping his hard-earned money or where necessity compels spending. Children should grow up seeing their father nurturing them in collaboration with the mother, not only for their immediate enjoyment, but for laying the foundation of their future families as well.

Men should learn how to give a listening ear to their wives. No matter how stupid a woman sounds, when a listening ear is given, the man will be able to get the necessary information, suggestion, or grievance that she is trying to pass. Because of lack of attention, some men may enter into trouble. Women have special eyes to see things more than the men, but it is left for men to listen attentively to whatever the women are saying. Moreover, the sensitivity of women plays a vital role in wellbeing of homes; actually, some may be so hyper, but a stich on time can save many where attention is fully given.

Reliability: The aim of every woman is to get shielded by her husband. That is why it takes a while for a lady to accept a proposal from the opposite sex. Among the qualities in search before saying yes, is reliability. It includes a good and stable job, housing, and other luxuries of life that will allow a couple to live comfortably. Again, among the other aspects of reliability is the full assurance that may come; the man will not cease being beside the lady.

In the journey of life, there is need for a stronger shoulder to lean on, especially women who are regarded as weak vessels, in view of that any woman who is lucky to hook up with the love of her life should rest assure that come rain or sunshine, she is standing secured. Where there are any lapses, the woman's entire personality is injured, therefore out of a sense of insecurity, she may develop some attitude that can derail the smooth movement of the home. Although being reliable does not include condoning nonsense of supporting irrelevant spending or wastage, but it means been there when most needed. Ability to provide necessity is a sign of reliability.

Caring: Jesus Christ, the coming king and the husband of the church, when he had completed his course on Earth, asked Simon Peter three times if he really loved him in John 21:17. He asked, "Simon, son of John, do you love me?" "Feed my sheep."

The action of Simon Peter was astonishing, indeed, that could be the response of everyone when there is confidence and genuineness of actions as in loving someone whole heartedly. He told Jesus, "Lord, you know I love you." This simple but holy conversation can be likened to the attitude of the father of a bride, giving his daughter out in marriage. Walking down the aisle holding the daughter's hand, and eventually handing over the daughter to the bridegroom, it will be noticed that usually the father always looks at the bridegroom straight to the face with that rhetoric question, especially the question Jesus Christ asked Peter. As a matter of fact, Jesus knew what would happen to the church after his death, unlike the bride's father who has no clue of what the future holds for his beautiful daughter.

In view of this, any man after taking up the responsibility of loving his wife at the point of knotting the tie, will not only hurt his wife but also her father where he fails to fulfill his promise. It is obvious that one can only care for what he loves. Therefore, caring for the wife and children in the house is a task given to man by God and man. When Jesus says "Feed my sheep" he knew there are grasses everywhere for sheep to feed on, yet he entrusted the care of the disciples and the whole followers then to Peter's hand for assurance of unity, love, and harmony.

A man must love his wife's parents first to really show genuine love in his home. A reasonable man will view the extent of damage his action could cause in the family of his wife, his own family, and the drastic effects of his children before putting up any action that can ruin his life. Where two elephants fight, the grass always suffers. Hence, the efforts of some men in consulting their parents, both sides when unexpected, begin to evolve.

Caring for the wife includes spiritual, financial, emotional, and moral. No religion allows unruly attitude towards the marriage vows. Honoring your wife and showing love to her is non-negotiable, because it is a choice that no one can make for a man. That is why many men shift the blame of the short-coming to either their parents, friends, or matchmakers on marriages that are arranged by the third party when they experience dissatisfaction in the home. Be it as it may, it is still expected of the man to take good care of their wives, notwithstanding how, where, or who is behind its formation. The level of care shown to a woman before she begins to make babies will determine the level it grows to when the coast is been expanding.

CHAPTER 9
Way Forward

Having charged the couple with their various duties and marital obligations and expectations, Dr. Richardson asked the couple whether they would be able to work in line with them. He was happy to hear them answering positively. He realized that they both love each other, and above all, they endured the treatment period in togetherness.

He asked the man, Mr. Lawson, if he had any question to ask. Mr. Lawson responded by craving for the forgiveness from his wife for taking the ignorant step of having a son from another woman. He wanted to know if it would be possible for his wife to living peacefully with the boy or not. Mrs. Lawson in tears had her eyes fixed to the roof of the office, she was quiet for a while and without looking at anyone said she had no problem living with the boy from the very day he came to join her family, after all, he was introduced initially as a cousin to her husband. But her concern is about his mother. She continued in her speech, "I cannot stand the madness of rivalry."

The husband quickly cut in, "No Dear, she had married another man, she has about two other children now."

By virtue of that, Mr. & Mrs. Lawson were made to fill an undertaking form in respect of peaceful cohabitation with the boy in their home. The form was scheduled to have legal backing to support the co-existence. Mr. Lawson vowed to treat his wife more honorable in his home, more than ever before, because of the way she maturely overlooked his mistake, and the sincere love she had been showing the boy even when she was unaware of his biological affiliation with the family.

Dr. Richardson asked if the boy was old

enough to be involved in signing the undertaking, although he was under-aged, so it was suggested that Mr. Lawson's mother should be made a witness since she played a vital role in arranging the mistress for her son. All the processes were eventually completed and necessary steps were duly followed.

Going through the history of the couple and related highlighted observation from their family friend, Dr. Richardson knew what advice to give them for proper repair of the marital damage. Childlessness was the major cause of the problem; he had the opinion that Mrs. Lawson was not a barren since she only miscarried the first ever. He advised them to reactivate their medical check-up with another medical practitioner who is completely new to them. The idea was welcomed, and they promised to do so as soon as possible.

Secondly, Dr. Richardson, being a Therapist with a wide knowledge of Family Therapy, applied one of his sure strategies. He is so confidence about the strategy to the extent that he always assured couples if they genuinely follow it through the restoration is always fast and effective. He asked them, "Where did you first meet?"

They told him that they met at a Christian Camp somewhere around the neighboring villages some years ago. He asked if the camp was still existing, and they said yes. He told them to find a time, in a short while, to revisit the camp for a weekend, just them. Initially, it sounded weird because they could not relate camping to family unrest. Sensing their confusion, the Therapist said, "I know you may be wondering what that has to do with your present situation, but I tell you, that very spot where you first met will bring back your lost affection, once you step there. Make it like a vacation break, you will thank me later."

He gave them the printout of the highlighted observations of their family friends, and the guidelines of expectations from Her to Him and from Him to Her. He insisted they should go with those and their Bible to meditate upon and to see where each one of them had missed their responsibilities, and to amend their ways.

The best ways to mend a broken gate is to gather the rubbles and reuse the valuables to make a strong fortified wall. Mr. & Mrs. Lawson left no stone unturned as regards the medical intervention, then proceeded on three days alone with God at the same camp where fate crossed their paths before becoming a couple. The three days were like a thousand night as they engaged in fervent prayers, walking around the Campground holding hands, chasing themselves, and implored all the available activities that extremely took their mind away from the usual stress that drew a very wide line between them during their storming moments.

A Few weeks after their short vacation, things began to change in the home. Mrs. Lawson looked at her husband one night and said, "Honey, look at you, you are adding more weight!"

Smiling, the husband replied by saying, "I

thought you're the only one that is looking more radiant these days; well thank God I am eating healthy nowadays since you resumed back to the kitchen." He said further, "Please, what do we have to eat now? I don't want to enter your office."

Oh wow! The therapy is working efficiently.

The early joy and affection of marriage suddenly reactivated, praying together, going places together, and eating together reappeared with full force. Unlike before, the siblings from both sides were happy to spend holidays and weekends with their brother and sister, most especially, the parents-in-laws.

One day a friend came and was so conscious of what could happen based on his past experience, but he was surprised to see the love and affection that the couple expressed to themselves in his presence. He was forced to say, "Oh God, it could only be you."

Mr. & Mrs. Benson were the happiest

friend ever after the good times started rolling in their friend's home. Because of that successful move, helping couples with domestic problem, and leading them to a marriage therapist for professional intervention became their ministry, a job they enjoyed doing.

Three months after the intervention, medical supports, and the visit to the Campground, Mrs. Lawson complained of general body pain, headache, and nauseating. Initially, it was thought to be the change of environment at the campground; nevertheless, the husband suggested seeing their family Doctor. After a series of medical tests, she was confirmed pregnant with twins, a boy and a girl. The news was a joy unlimited. They kept it secret from everyone until the pregnancy was six months and it could no longer be hidden.

The first person to comment was Mrs. Benson, who had never stopped praying for her friend. The two couples then engaged themselves in full warfare to ensure safety delivery of the twins. Mr. Lawson's mother saw it, but she was not allowed to bring any cultural idea that could bring any other problem to the family.

The twins came. It was a story of a great battle won. Within five years, the couple had five beautiful children to the glory of God. Mr. Lawson's first son was just a sent angel to the family; he assisted his stepmother in no small measure to raise and nurture his siblings; they were all happy together because no one could believe that Mrs. Lawson was not his mother.

It is not a crime to fall but staying there is worst. The family went through the challenges for several years before the intervention of their friend, the therapist, and the medical Doctor, and with God on their sides they sailed through the storm. There are many families that could not survive such predicaments or lack of knowing the source, or the way out like the above couple. Marital toss is always likely to occur, especially at the beginning of the journey, but the victory depends on how quickly the course is discovered and knowing the prompt way out.

TO GOD BE THE GLORY